DANGEROUS DRUGS

VICODIN AND OXYCONTIN

CHRISTINE PETERSEN

Cavendish
Square
New York

Published in 2014 by Cavendish Square Publishing, LLC
303 Park Avenue South, Suite 1247, New York, NY 10010

LIBRARY OF CONGRESS CATALOGING-IN-PUBLICATION DATA
Petersen, Christine.
Vicodin and OxyContin / Christine Petersen.
p. cm. — (Dangerous drugs)
Summary: "Provides comprehensive information on the dangers of Vicodin and OxyContin abuse"—
Provided by publisher.
Includes bibliographical references and index.
ISBN 978-1-60870-827-7 (hardcover) ISBN 978-1-62712-063-0 (paperback)
ISBN 978-1-60870-833-8 (ebook)
1. Narcotics—Juvenile literature. 2. Drug addiction—Juvenile literature. I. Title. II. Series.
RC566.P45 2013
616.86_32—dc23
2011027729

EDITOR: Christine Florie   ART DIRECTOR: Anahid Hamparian   SERIES DESIGNER: Kristen Branch

EXPERT READER: Lewis S. Nelson, MD, associate professor, Department of Emergency Medicine,
NYU Emergency Medicine Associates, New York, New York

Photo research by Marybeth Kavanagh

Cover photo by Presselect/Alamy
The photographs in this book are used by permission and through the courtesy of: *SuperStock*: The Copyright Group, 4; Belinda Images, 17; age fotostock, 41; Kablonk, 53; Erik Isakson/Blend Images, 55; *Photo Researchers, Inc.*: Medi-Mation Ltd, 7; *Getty Images*: Photo Researchers, 8L; Rex Ziak/Stone, 43; altrendo images, 49; *AP Photo*: Toby Talbot, 8R; Steven Senne, 22; *Alamy*: Nigel Cattlin, 10; joefoxphoto, 35; *Newscom*: Kathryn Indiek/ZUMAPRESS, 19L; Maria Ramirez, 19R; Eduardo Arrivabene/Splash News, 26; Odilon Dimier/Altopress, 29; Custom Medical Stock Photo, 31; *Corbis*: Boris Roessler/dpa, 40; Kurt Rogers/San Francisco Chronicle, 46   Most subjects in these photos are models.

Printed in the United States of America

CONTENTS

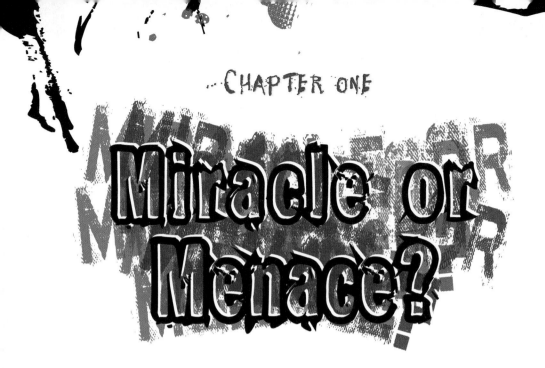

CHAPTER ONE

Miracle or Menace?

"**P**AIN IS SUCH AN UNCOMFORTABLE FEEL-ing that even a tiny amount of it is enough to ruin every enjoyment." The famed cowboy actor Will Rogers made this comment almost a century ago. His plain words say a lot about the power of pain. Pain is more than a physical experience. It has the potential to invade the mind, heart, and soul. Perhaps this is why people have always looked for ways to make pain go away.

Although pain can make a person miserable, it serves an important purpose. Pain is a warning system. It is an

Left: Pain cannot be seen by others, yet it is something many people experience due to injury or illness.

alarm signaling that something is wrong within the body or affecting it from the outside. Touch a hot pan on the stove, and nerves in your skin instantly send signals to your brain. The signals travel along the complex network of nerves leading from the skin on your hand to your spinal cord and brain. Within milliseconds, your brain processes this information, and your hand pulls back rapidly.

Modern medicine offers many options for pain relief. Mild pain is treated with **nonprescription analgesics**, which ease pain without causing sleepiness. Adults can purchase aspirin, acetaminophen, and ibuprofen over the counter at pharmacies and other stores. These drugs are used to relieve a headache, a fever caused by a cold, or muscle aches after a hard workout. **Opioid** analgesics (also known as opioids) are a separate group of painkillers. These drugs are made from the juice of the **opium** poppy or are made in a laboratory from opium-like chemicals. Opioids control pain by mimicking **endorphins**, a group of chemicals naturally produced when the body begins to feel pain. Endorphins bind to dock-like receptor sites found in the brain and spinal cord. When the docks are filled—either by endorphins or by opioid chemicals— the feeling of pain eases. Because opioid drugs are so

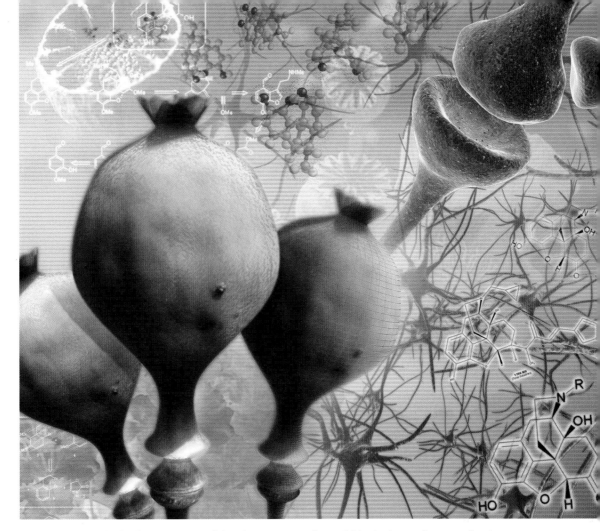

Opioid chemicals (red at top center) bind to nerve cells and block the pathways of pain signals. They are highly addictive. Green opium pods are depicted on the left.

powerful, they are generally legally available only with a doctor's prescription.

Vicodin and OxyContin are two of the most commonly prescribed opioids available today. Under the supervision of a doctor, these and similar drugs are prescribed for patients with serious pain-related problems. Yet Vicodin

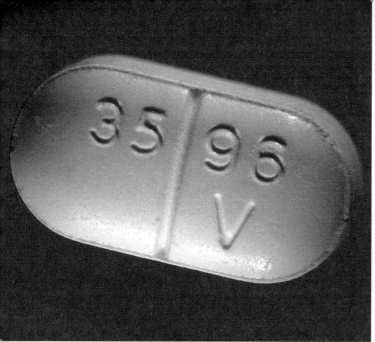
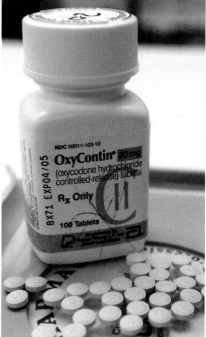

Vicodin (left) and OxyContin (right) are two of the most commonly misused prescription painkillers in the United States.

and OxyContin are also among the nation's most abused prescription drugs. They have the power to turn a healthy person's life into a nightmare.

THE FIRST PAINKILLER

Although Vicodin and OxyContin have been available for just a few decades, chemically they are similar to opium, the world's oldest known painkilling drug. Modern researchers have found stone tablets describing how the Sumerians obtained opium from poppy flowers more than five thousand years ago. Travelers and traders eventually brought this drug to Egypt, Greece, India, and China.

8

NAME-CALLING

Your parents or guardians may be the ones buying and dispensing medications for you right now. But in a few years, you'll be responsible for your own health care. It's important to learn about drug safety and to understand the language used by doctors and pharmacists to describe different types of health care products.

Brand-name products are specific products made by particular manufacturers. New drugs must be approved by the U.S. Food and Drug Administration (FDA). If the FDA determines that a drug is safe and effective, the manufacturer can choose a name and begin selling the drug to pharmacies. The brand-name nonprescription analgesics Tylenol, Motrin, and Aleve are recognized by many. Vicodin and OxyContin are two of the many brand-name opioids currently available.

After a brand-name drug has been on the market for twenty years, other drug manufacturers are allowed to develop generic versions of that same drug. Generic drugs are referred to by their chemical names. The generic name for Tylenol is acetaminophen. The generic for Motrin is ibuprofen. Vicodin contains two generic drugs: an opioid called hydrocodone plus acetaminophen. OxyContin's generic is known as oxycodone.

If the pharmacist fills your prescription with a generic drug, you can be confident it will work as well as the brand-name equivalent. However, you should never assume it's safe to try a drug because it's "just a generic." Hydrocodone and oxycodone may not be brand names, but they are powerful drugs. A drug—whatever it's called—should never be taken unless that medication was prescribed by a physician.

An opium poppy flower pod leaks white sap, which when dried to solid resin is known as opium.

Long ago, healers discovered that opium had many uses beyond the relief of pain. The drug eased patients to sleep, controlled coughs, and stopped diarrhea.

Diocles of Carystos, a Greek who lived in the fourth century BCE, wrote the following about opium:

There is much that is still unknown about this wondrous flower. The potion prepared from its capsule will soothe some but cast others into melancholy. . . . In some the medication will be well tolerated. In others it will have unpleasant side effects. Yet even when it does not abolish pain, the pain no longer preys on the person's mind.

Diocles wanted his readers to understand that opium caused unpredictable side effects. On the one hand, it can reduce anxiety and fear and create a feeling of well-being and relaxation. In this state, a patient can forget about his or her pain. Opium also has a dark side, however. Users may become depressed and often experience nausea,

10

vomiting, and constipation. The **addictive** nature of the drug creates physical and mental cravings that users find almost impossible to ignore. Opium can also be toxic; a user may unexpectedly end up in a coma or possibly even die after a single use. Past kings and military leaders knew of opium's deadly characteristics—that just the right dose could cause a person's breathing to slow until it stopped. Hence the poison was used to kill enemies.

Ibn Sina, an eleventh-century Persian physician, learned these lessons the hard way. For many years, he prescribed opium for his patients to treat a wide range of medical complaints. Yet historical records suggest that Ibn Sina himself was addicted to the drug and may have died accidentally after drinking opium mixed with wine.

Acute or Chronic?

Opium is no longer considered safe, and its use has been banned in the United States. Instead physicians can choose from many different opioids, including Vicodin and OxyContin, depending on the patient's type of pain. Hydrocodone (found in Vicodin) was developed to treat the **acute pain** that accompanies many injuries and diseases. The acute pain felt after spraining an ankle, burning a hand, or having a tooth pulled lessens over time. If a doctor prescribes Vicodin or another drug containing hydrocodone, the dose will be reduced as the patient heals. Within a few days or weeks, the patient is expected to stop using the drug.

In contrast, **chronic pain** often lasts for weeks, months, or years. This type of pain is associated with cancer, joint diseases (such as arthritis), back injuries, and other long-term health problems. It does not typically improve over time. To treat chronic pain, physicians often prescribe drugs containing oxycodone. OxyContin is unique among opioids because it is formulated to release slowly in the digestive tract. Instead of providing quick but short-lived pain relief, OxyContin provides patients with pain relief for up to twelve hours.

Diocles warned that there were risks when using opium, and the same is true of opioids. Vicodin and OxyContin—like many opioids—are highly addictive and toxic in large doses. These drugs may also cause the user's breathing to slow down so much that death results from lack of oxygen. Despite the hazards, some people find opium and opioids tempting—even when they have no medical reason to use them. To some young people,

the high that comes from using painkillers seems like a harmless form of recreation. Others have found that these drugs make emotional pain easier to bear. They use drugs to relieve the stress of life's challenges.

Do you know someone who has tried Vicodin or Oxy-Contin? In a 2010 study called Monitoring the Future, conducted by the University of Michigan in Ann Arbor, one in twelve high school seniors said he or she had tried Vicodin. Five percent (one in twenty) had used OxyContin, which is one of the strongest opioids available. Even middle school–aged kids are experimenting with these powerful drugs. Most young people—and many adults—have no idea that opioids are addictive and potentially deadly.

CHAPTER TWO

A Good Time?

YOU AND A FRIEND ARE INVITED TO A party hosted by a classmate you've been eager to hang out with. You're a little surprised to find that there's no adult home to supervise, but things seem to be under control, so you decide to stay for a little while. You talk to some old friends, get to know a couple of new people, dance, and have a snack. Then comes the chance you've been waiting for. The host sits down beside you on the couch. You are getting along really well—and then he offers you a selection of pills. "It's only Vike and OC," he says, using the street names for Vicodin and OxyContin. "Everyone does it. The buzz is awesome!"

Have you ever been asked by classmates to participate in activities that break the rules or seem risky? Or have you felt you were expected to look, dress, or behave differently to fit in? That's peer pressure. Many kids say that their first drug use was the result of peer pressure. It's hard to say no when you want to make friends—or when you fear being bullied for refusing.

Peer pressure is a powerful force. Adults feel it, too. Yet it's important to weigh the costs of giving in, especially when it comes to drugs. Give it some thought, and you will probably realize that a worthwhile friend would never push you to do something dangerous or illegal. If you still feel unsure, here are some good reasons to avoid Vicodin and OxyContin.

It Could Happen to You

Teens may assume that it's safe to use Vicodin and OxyContin because these drugs are available legally by prescription (unlike marijuana, cocaine, and other **illicit drugs**). If a doctor ordered the drug for one of your family members, it can't be dangerous—right? Nothing could be further from the truth. Healthy people are not meant to use Vicodin or OxyContin.

A doctor's prescription for these medicines is based on knowledge of the patient's health status, weight, and medical history. The doctor also considers which other drugs the patient is taking at the time. In other words, the dose is customized especially for one person's needs. Patients taking Vicodin and OxyContin are typically counseled about proper use of the drug. They must take the prescription exactly as ordered to avoid problems. The doctor also warns about developing a **tolerance**. With regular use, the patient's body slowly adapts to the effects of Vicodin or OxyContin. Gradually, that dose becomes less effective. A higher level of medication may be required in order to control the pain. At this point, a patient can work with his or her physician to find a new dose that will be safe and effective. In time, a patient being treated for chronic pain may develop a tolerance for even a very high dose of the medication.

Now imagine yourself facing a handful of pills back at that party. By sight alone, you may not be able to tell what drug is being offered, let alone what dose—low or extremely high. (OxyContin pills range from 10 to 80 milligrams, meaning some doses are eight times stronger than others.) A person who has not built up a tolerance

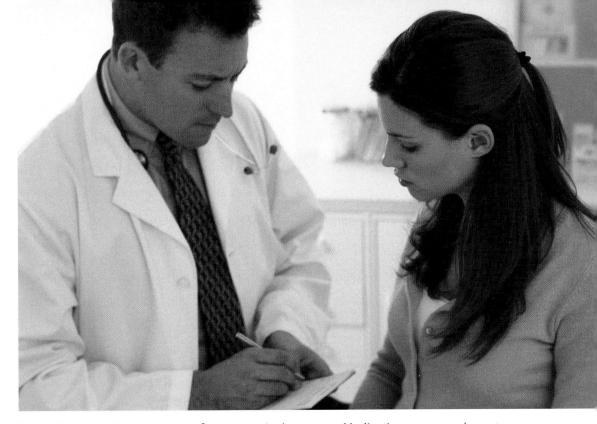

Doctors' prescriptions are meant for one particular person. Medication can cause harm to those it is not prepared for.

for Vicodin or OxyContin, by taking a single pill, could trigger an **overdose**.

An opioid overdose causes confused behavior and feelings of extreme drowsiness. The victim's pupils **constrict** and become so narrow that they look like black pinpricks in the center of the eyes. The skin may grow cold and sweaty. These symptoms can come on very suddenly and may be deadly if not treated immediately.

Opioids produce a calm, sleepy feeling in the user by slowing down breathing. Doctors have a name for this condition: respiratory depression. This is the most dangerous sign of overdose. Alcohol, **barbiturates**, and antihistamines (over-the-counter allergy and cold medicines) are also **depressants**. All the substances a person consumes interact (mix) in the bloodstream and nervous system. One chemical may strengthen the side effects of another. Can you predict what happens when you combine two or more depressants? Your lungs, brain, and other organs require oxygen to function. Deprived of this essential source of energy, you may slip into a coma or die.

This kind of mixing contributed to the deaths of the actors Heath Ledger and Brittany Murphy. Ledger, only twenty-eight at the time of his death in 2008, had been taking opioids similar to Vicodin and OxyContin, as well as antianxiety drugs and sleep medications. Less than two years later, the thirty-two-year-old Murphy died while using Vicodin along with a variety of medications to treat cold-like symptoms. There were no signs that either actor intended to commit suicide. Like many people, they probably had no idea of the serious consequences of drug interactions.

According to the Drug Abuse Warning Network, in 2008 more than 4.3 million people made drug-related

Actors Heath Ledger and Brittany Murphy died after taking opioid painkillers along with other medications.

visits to emergency rooms in the United States. At least 20 percent of these resulted from abuse of Vicodin, Oxy-Contin, and similar opioids.

Hidden Dangers

Overdose and interactions can be a problem when using almost any drug, but Vicodin and OxyContin have particularly unique dangers.

PUTTING DRUGS ON A SCHEDULE

Concerns about drug abuse led Congress to pass the Controlled Substances Act of 1970 (CSA). The CSA put two federal agencies in charge of drug-abuse prevention. The FDA makes sure that prescription and over-the-counter medications are safe before Americans use them. The Drug Enforcement Agency (DEA) works to prevent drug abuse, smuggling from other countries, and drug theft within the United States.

The FDA assigned each drug to one of five levels on a drug schedule. Schedule I drugs have no accepted uses for medical treatment. They are sometimes called illicit, street, or recreational drugs. Federal law has made all uses of these drugs illegal. Each state determines specific punishments for using, possessing, buying, or selling them. Drugs on Schedules II through V are currently used in medical treatment. Because some of these drugs are abused, states enforce laws targeting preventing their abuse and theft.

- Schedule I—These drugs are considered highly addictive and potentially harmful to users' health. Examples include heroin, LSD, methamphetamines, and marijuana.

- Schedule II—When abused, these drugs can be highly addictive. OxyContin and morphine are on this list, along with amphetamines, Ritalin, and some barbiturates.
- Schedule III—These drugs also hold a risk for addiction. Examples include Vicodin and anabolic steroids.
- Schedule IV—Risk for addiction with these drugs, though lower than with those higher up the schedule, remains a possibility. Xanax, Ambien, Ativan, and a variety of diet drugs are on this list.
- Schedule V—Abuse is less common with these drugs. Codeine is on this list, but in very low doses and mixed with ingredients that are not addictive.

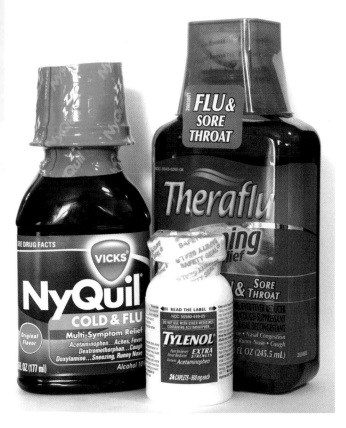

These over-the-counter medications all contain acetaminophen, which when taken in large amounts can cause liver damage.

As stated earlier, Vicodin contains two drugs: hydrocodone and acetaminophen. Most people consider acetaminophen a harmless drug. It's available in many over-the-counter medicines for adults and children. In recent years mounting evidence suggests that acetaminophen causes liver damage. As a result, representatives of the FDA have become concerned about the health of frequent users of this drug. Especially at risk are those taking multiple drugs containing acetaminophen. For example, anyone using (or abusing) Vicodin while taking over-the-counter headache or cold remedies would be exposed to very high doses of the drug.

The FDA thought of banning Vicodin. With no other drug available to provide relief for acute pain, however, the FDA looked for a compromise. Drug manufacturers were asked to limit the dose of acetaminophen in

over-the-counter and opioid analgesic medications to 325 milligrams by 2014. Drug companies were also asked to provide a written warning with every prescription to inform users that acetaminophen can cause severe liver damage. Reducing the dose of acetaminophen is no guarantee of safety. Those who choose to take Vicodin are still at serious risk of liver damage. This vital organ cleans impurities from the blood.

When it was first approved for sale in the United States in 1995, OxyContin seemed like a miracle drug for people with chronic pain. Its twelve-hour, extended-release formula kept pain from flaring up repeatedly throughout the day and allowed patients to sleep better at night. Even more important, OxyContin's controlled-release formula seemed to reduce the risk of addiction. This feature depended on the pills being taken whole. Those taking the drug for a fast and powerful high would crush OxyContin pills and then swallow or sniff the powder or dissolve it in water and use needles to inject the solution. In powder form, the entire dose is released at once. The resulting high was extremely addictive and sometimes deadly.

In 2010 a new type of OxyContin pill was developed. A new ingredient now ensures that OxyContin will only dissolve when exposed to liquids, such as those found within the stomach. Under those conditions, the medication becomes a gel rather than a powder—it can't be snorted. If abusers soak the pills, they find the sticky substance hard to inject. This formula does not decrease the risk of OxyContin addiction or overdose, but it will discourage some people from abusing the drug.

Friends may tell you that it's no big deal to try Vicodin or OxyContin. The facts suggest otherwise. Make up your own mind. Weigh the risks before you pop a pill.

CHAPTER THREE

The Danger Zone

PEOPLE DON'T PLAN TO BECOME addicted when they try Vicodin or OxyContin. Yet too often that opioid high draws people to repeat the experience. Use may begin as a casual social activity at parties and then escalate to a regular habit, whether or not friends join in.

Years ago, it was believed that people could quit drugs anytime they wanted. Those who failed were considered weak willed. Now experts understand that addiction is very complex. It happens on many levels—physical, mental, and emotional. Vicodin, OxyContin, and other prescription painkillers actually change the chemistry of a user's body. The only way to be sure of not becoming addicted to these

Jack Osbourne (right), the son of rock star Ozzy Osbourne (left), suffered from an addiction to Vicodin and OxyContin.

drugs is never to take them. The best way for a user to quit is with the support of loved ones and medical professionals.

Jack's Story

From the outside, Jack Osbourne seemed to have a perfect life. The son of the heavy metal rocker Ozzy Osbourne was on a popular reality television series. He lived in a big house, had lots of independence, and was invited to celebrity-filled parties. But this lifestyle also exposed the teen to many temptations. Jack had begun drinking and smoking marijuana in middle school. Within a couple of years, he was abusing Vicodin and OxyContin.

At first Jack liked the way OxyContin made him feel. It seemed to help him deal with the stress he felt when fans criticized him and when he found out his mother had cancer. Eventually the teen's life hit a low point.

After attempting suicide, Jack finally admitted to his mother that he was abusing opioids. He entered the adolescent psychiatric ward of a Los Angeles hospital.

Jack had a lot of work to do in order to get healthy. He had become **dependent** on opioids to feel normal, both physically and emotionally. Jack first had to go through **withdrawal**. This is a period of time during which the body adjusts to not having the drug. The earliest sign of withdrawal is often a craving—a strong desire to take the drug. This is followed by physical signs such as sweating, yawning, a runny nose, and watery eyes. The body continues to show its need through sleeplessness, bad temper, and loss of appetite. Depending on how long the person has been dependent and how large the usual dose was, he or she may also suffer nausea and vomiting. Chills, fever, and muscle spasms can wrack the body for days. Withdrawal is never the end of the story for people, like Jack, who have abused Vicodin or OxyContin for a long time. They may continue to fight that craving for months or even years.

Once the drugs had been cleansed from Jack's system, he spent several months in an inpatient drug **rehabilitation** (rehab) facility. Here, Jack met other young people who were also trying to overcome addiction. He talked with counselors to discover what made him vulnerable to drug abuse. His family sometimes joined the discussion. He also met in groups with other kids in the program.

This kind of honest self-exploration was an important part of Jack's recovery. His father had been through rehab fourteen times. Jack knew that if he wanted to remain sober, he would have to accept the fact that recovery is a lifelong process. Success requires inner strength to deal with life's challenges, as well as the development of a set of skills to resist drugs and alcohol in the future.

Michael's Story

Not every person who tries Vicodin or OxyContin will become addicted. The problem is that addiction is unpredictable. It can happen to anyone—a movie star or a high school track star, a lumber mill worker or a middle school student who babysits on weekends. Drug dependence often creeps up slowly, and people may not recognize that they have a problem.

Michael R. is not a celebrity. He's an active young man with friends and diverse interests. A few years ago, as he was about to graduate from high school, Michael realized that he was scared and uncertain. He couldn't picture what life

would hold for him in the future. As a distraction, Michael began to use OxyContin with friends.

Michael's addiction to Oxy-Contin changed his personality and behavior. His older sister, Caitlin, couldn't help noticing when her easygoing brother began to treat family members differently. After a while, the family began to realize that money was missing. Michael recalls that his OxyContin habit was extremely expensive—as much as $70 for a single 80-milligram pill. Addiction had taken him to the point that most people believe they will never reach. He was steal-

Drug addiction may lead to uncharacteristic behavior, such as stealing money to pay for drugs.

ing cash and selling off his own belongings to pay for the drugs. Michael's situation was common among abusers of this expensive, addictive drug.

At first, OxyContin seemed to make his worries melt away. Before long, however, Michael realized the drug was in control of him. He wanted to quit using but found it physically painful whenever the drug began to leave his system. The pain, anxiety, and depression of withdrawal are severe enough to send many people back to opioid abuse. Surviving withdrawal usually requires a strong will, support from others, and medical assistance—and that's just the beginning of the recovery process.

When a friend overdosed on OxyContin, Michael decided to ask for help. After talking to his mother, he joined an outpatient treatment program. Like rehab, outpatient treatment involves regular counseling. The individual may speak privately with a therapist or meet with family to work through shared problems. Peer groups help teens build a support system made up of people with a similar experience. Outpatient treatment allows a person to stay at home and carry on with daily life—work, school, and family responsibilities. It's less expensive than inpatient treatment but requires extra dedication to be successful. The person in recovery must stick to a program every day.

A Little Help

Some people need more than therapy to break from the stranglehold of Vicodin or OxyContin addiction. In addition to counseling, they can receive drug therapy,

which controls the powerful cravings that may still nag at the addict. Several options are available, but all must be undertaken under the care of a trained physician.

More than thirty years ago methadone was the first drug used to treat opioid addiction. Another treatment, Suboxone (also called buprenorphine), has helped Michael stay free of his addiction since January 2009. Both of these drugs are effective because they work in the brain much as opioids do. The chemical binds to and changes receptors in the nervous system. There are three major benefits:

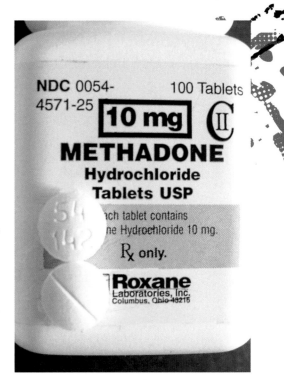

Methadone is a well-tested medication used for the treatment of painkiller withdrawal and addiction.

- The person feels neither a craving for the drug nor withdrawal symptoms.
- If the person takes any kind of opioid, the drug will have no effect because the receptors are already occupied.
- If used properly, the drug causes no high.

The effects of methadone and Suboxone last about a day. Patients in treatment must remember never to miss a dose, or their drug craving is likely to return. In the case of methadone, patients must visit a clinic daily to receive their medication.

A drawback to methadone and Suboxone use is the risk of addiction, which may result if the drugs are misused. To provide an option, in 2010 the FDA approved a new drug for treatment of opioid addiction. Vivitrol is given by injection, and its effects last for a month. There appears to be no threat of addiction to Vivitrol, but it is very expensive. At approximately $1,100 per treatment, many patients may be unable to afford this option.

At Risk

In 2010 the DEA released a report showing the number of Americans who went to rehab for addiction to Vicodin, OxyContin, and related prescription painkillers. Between 1998 and 2008, the number of rehab admissions increased by 400 percent. Even the experts were troubled to see that the problem had gotten out of control. "Our national prescription drug abuse problem cannot be ignored," said A. Thomas McLellan, deputy director at the Office of National Drug

You Can Make a Difference

Outpatient therapy is most effective when the individuals have a support group—family or friends who can help them stay strong. That's certainly true in Michael R.'s case. After he entered treatment in January 2009, Michael's sister and two cousins started an advocacy group on Facebook called Bring Awareness to Maryland's OxyContin Epidemic. The founders of this group have a simple but powerful mission. "It's time we show our neighbors we love them," they say, "and demand more attention to the OxyContin epidemic." Although none of these young people are experts on drug addiction or recovery, they seek to help people understand its risks and ways to avoid the problem. Social media, such as Facebook, allows people who live in different parts of the country or around the world to share ideas and experiences. It can be a very effective tool when used responsibly.

This particular Facebook group may exist for only a few years, but it's a good example of what people can accomplish when they care about a cause. If you feel strongly about drug abuse prevention, join with others in your school, neighborhood, or religious community. Spread the word that it's cool to choose a drug-free lifestyle.

Control Policy. "I have worked in the treatment field for the last thirty-five years, and recent trends regarding the extent of prescription drug abuse are startling." Preventing opioid abuse is made more difficult because the problem cannot be traced to any particular group of Americans. Prescription painkillers are abused by the young and the old, males and females, the rich and the poor, as well as people of all races and ethnicities.

However, there are a few factors that seem to put certain individuals at greater risk of using opioids. Stress is high on the list. Young people may seek to numb the emotions that go along with life's challenges, such as parental divorce or pressure to perform well in school or sports. Loss of a loved one, moving to a new house or town, and neglect or abuse also lead some kids to try drugs. According to an annual study conducted by the Partnership for a Drug-Free America, girls are more likely than boys to believe that drugs will ease stress. The Partnership's 2009 survey reveal-ed that "[m]ore than two-thirds of teen girls responded positively to the question 'using drugs helps kids deal with problems at home' . . . and more than half reported that drugs help teens forget their troubles." Boys said that they use drugs as a way to relax socially.

34

Stress, anxiety, and a desire to fit in with peers are among the many factors that contribute to drug abuse among teens.

In a family biography, Ozzy Osbourne pointed out another reason why some people are prone to addiction. Pondering his son Jack's struggle with OxyContin, Osbourne said, "It might also be genetic. It might be the ticking time bomb he inherited from me. You never know what drink or which drug is going to set it off." The evidence that he may have been right grew stronger in 2004, when Osbourne's daughter Kelly also admitted to years of opioid abuse. But there is a way to beat that "time bomb" if addiction seems to run in your family: if you are offered drugs or alcohol, make a choice to say no every time. You can't change your genes, but you are in charge of your behavior.

CHAPTER FOUR

This Is Your Life

A PICTURE IS BEGINNING TO EMERGE IN your mind as you see all the negative outcomes of Vicodin and OxyContin abuse. The choices you make today have a big impact on your health and your future.

The Centers for Disease Control and Prevention (CDC) conducts a long-term study called the Youth Risk Behavior Surveillance (YRBS). Surveys are given to students at public and private high schools across the United States. Teens rank their behavior in particular categories, including

- activities that contribute to unintentional injuries and violence

- tobacco use
- alcohol and other drug use
- sexual-risk behaviors
- unhealthy dietary behaviors
- physical activity

The CDC states, "Results from the 2009 national YRBS indicated that many high school students are engaged in behaviors that increase their likelihood for the leading causes of death among persons aged 10–24 years in the United States." Teens reported failing to wear seat belts, driving while intoxicated, fighting, and having unprotected sex, along with many other risky behaviors. In addition, more than 20 percent of students said they had taken prescription drugs (such as Vicodin and OxyContin) without a doctor's prescription.

Once established, these habits are hard to change, and bad habits are a slippery slope. One risky behavior tends to lead to another. The good news is that a person can make good choices and avoid the slippery slope. Staying away from drugs and alcohol is a great start. A clear head will help a person stay in control of his or her life. You can choose what kind of life you want to live.

Not in the Plan

When people take certain drugs, their usual worries and self-consciousness may seem to fall away. It's a side effect that attracts many people to use for the first time. However, under the influence of Vicodin, OxyContin, and other opioids, you are more vulnerable and less able to think clearly. This makes it easy for other people to take advantage of you—for example, to convince or force you to have sex. This may lead to pregnancy or sexually transmitted diseases.

There's another, far more dangerous consequence that may occur if you choose to take drugs with a needle. According to the CDC, "In 2007, injection-drug use was the third most frequently reported risk factor among persons with diagnosed human immunodeficiency virus (HIV) infection in the United States." HIV is the virus that leads to acquired immune deficiency syndrome (AIDS). Although AIDS treatment has improved since the HIV virus was discovered thirty years ago, there remains no cure. AIDS ravages the body before it takes a victim's life. Approximately one-twelfth of all people diagnosed with HIV in the United States each year are injection drug users. They got the virus by sharing needles while using drugs such as OxyContin and heroin. During the

Blood-borne viruses such as HIV and hepatitis are often spread when needles are shared during drug use.

three-year period of 2004 to 2007, more than 7 percent of Americans who contracted HIV through injection drug use were young people under the age of twenty-four.

A Dark Road

Addiction makes good people do things they never imagined possible. Think of Michael R., whose OxyContin addiction led him to sell valued personal belongings and to steal money from his family. When desperate to obtain drugs, Vicodin and OxyContin abusers may also try "doctor shopping," where the addict visits several doctors and seeks a separate

prescription from each. Each prescription is then filled at a different pharmacy to reduce the risk of being caught. Addicts have also been known to forge (illegally write) prescriptions. Some buy drugs from dishonest pharmacists or other health care workers, who have stolen the drugs to make a profit.

When prescription painkillers are no longer affordable, addicts sometimes make the switch to heroin. The effects of this illicit drug are very similar to OxyContin's. The fact that heroin is usually taken by injection greatly increases the risk of contracting blood-borne diseases such as HIV and hepatitis B and C. Repeated injections of the drug can lead to a range of health problems, including pneumonia, infection of the heart, and liver or kidney disease. This Schedule I drug is not made in laboratories, and no one tests it for purity. Heroin may be cut with substances as harmless as sugar or as deadly as strychnine, a poison used to kill rats.

Some addicts move on to heroin when prescription painkillers are no longer accessible or affordable.

41

MAKE THE CONNECTION

The University of Michigan's Monitoring the Future study confirms that many young people would never consider using heroin. In 2010 more than 64 percent of high school seniors said it would be very dangerous to try heroin once or twice—even without using a needle. Yet there is a misunderstanding when it comes to prescription pain-killers. Young people—and adults—often don't understand that Vicodin and OxyContin are chemically similar to heroin. All of these drugs are dangerous and potentially addictive when abused.

When you're with friends, facing that choice of whether to try Vicodin or OxyContin, think about the possible consequences of your actions. It is illegal to use prescription drugs unless a physician ordered them for you as treatment for a real health problem. You can be arrested just for taking the drug once or having a pill in your possession. Buying or selling prescription drugs is even more serious. Those activities are illegal in every state and can lead to time in detention or prison.

The sentence depends on your age, the amount and kind of drugs involved, and any previous arrest record. But any arrest is a life-changing event. You may lose privileges at home, miss time at school, or be fired from a job. Drug use or an arrest can get you kicked off a sports team. It limits your choices for college and cuts off scholarships or grants you may need to get a higher education. As the CDC's Youth Risk Behavior Surveillance report clearly

Jail time is one serious consequence of using, selling, or possessing illegal prescription drugs.

shows, drug use is tied to many behaviors that increase the risk of death for teens. Vicodin and OxyContin abuse may steal your life in much more subtle ways. They take your health, your relationships, and even your freedom.

The facts are worth repeating. Opioids such as Vicodin and OxyContin are intended to treat medical conditions involving pain. Even then, it is only safe to take such drugs under certain conditions:

- if the drug has been prescribed specifically for you by a physician
- if you have received the drug from a legitimate pharmacy
- if you are using the drug exactly as prescribed (for example, not mixing drugs unless your physician has checked the interactions of the medications for safety)
- if you stop using the drug when it is no longer needed

Slowing the Flow

In a 2010 survey, more than two thousand teens nationwide were asked how quickly they could obtain a prescription drug.

Thirty-two percent said they could do so within a day. Of those, more than half believed it was possible to access a prescription drug in an hour or less. The accessibility of Vicodin and OxyContin make it very difficult to prevent drug abuse.

Governments and law enforcement play an important role in this effort. The federal government's "National Drug Control Strategy" has been written every year since 1988. It covers prevention and treatment, law enforcement, smuggling control, and sales of drugs within the United States. President Barack Obama's strategy has given special attention to drug abuse prevention. As part of this effort, in September 2010 the DEA sponsored the first annual national prescription drug Take Back campaign.

According to the DEA, "More than 70 percent of people who abuse prescription drugs get them from friends or family—often from the home medicine cabinet." Old prescription drugs may remain in the medicine cabinet because parents don't realize the risk or simply don't know how to get rid of them. The first Take Back program provided four thousand sites nationwide for safe disposal of prescription drugs. In a single day, more than 242,000 pounds (110,000 kilograms) of drugs were turned in.

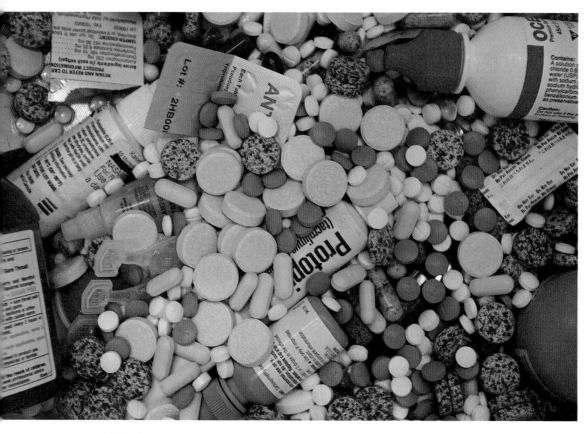

A bin full of expired prescription drugs is collected as part of the Take Back program, which educates Americans on how to properly dispose of expired or unused medications.

The DEA will continue to offer annual Take-Back events for several years. The plan is to educate people about the importance of proper drug disposal.

The focus of the Ryan Haight Online Pharmacy Consumer Protection Act of 2008 is to shut down Internet

pharmacies that sell Vicodin, OxyContin, and other drugs without valid prescriptions. The law is named for a teenager who died from a Vicodin overdose in 2001. Ryan Haight obtained a prescription from a doctor online and had it filled from an Internet pharmacy. His mother hopes the bill will protect other teens from a similar fate—and protect their families from a tragic loss. "Since Ryan's death, others have died after purchasing controlled drugs over the Internet," she writes. "Prescription drug usage is up among our teens. The passing of this Bill is a good place to start to protect our youth from having an easy way to get them."

Every opioid developed throughout history has been abused in one way or another. Yet governments cannot simply ban them. Painkilling drugs such as Vicodin and OxyContin are needed in medical treatment. Millions of people worldwide suffer acute or chronic pain as the result of serious health conditions. Drug abuse prevention really comes down to communities, families, and individuals. When people learn the risks and support each other in making healthy choices, everyone benefits.

CHAPTER FIVE

A Better Way

IT'S A TOUGH SCENARIO. YOUR FRIEND began using prescription painkillers a few months ago. At first it seemed harmless. Now the situation has gotten out of control. You hardly see your friend anymore because he spends more time with other classmates who use. The last couple of times you talked, he was impatient and hurtful. He looks tired and scruffy, and yesterday he quit the basketball team. You are worried about him. What do you do?

It's important to support friends through hard times, but addiction makes relationships complex. Vicodin and OxyContin change the chemistry of a user's brain. Your friend may do and say things he does not mean. The first

Lend support to a friend suffering with an addiction.

thing to remember is that you cannot "fix" a person who is addicted. He must be ready for recovery and will require professional help to get through that process. Nor is it healthy for you to get caught up in his situation. It won't benefit him if you provide money or lie to cover his drug use. If the situation gets out of control, you may need to tell an adult.

Along the way, you may need support—even if your friend doesn't choose to seek it. Contact Nar-Anon (see the Find Out More section in the back of this book) or find an organization in your community.

It's time to ask yourself a couple of questions. Have you ever tried Vicodin or OxyContin? If so, is there any chance you could have a problem with these drugs?

SELF-CHECK

It may be hard to recognize or admit your problems at first. You may fear punishment or have no idea how to begin asking for help. The first step is simply to acknowledge that you need help. If any of the following statements describe your behavior since beginning to use Vicodin, OxyContin, or any other drug, it's time to reach out.

☐ A large proportion of my money is spent on Vicodin (or OxyContin).

☐ I frequently think about the drug—how it feels to use it, where and when I can next take it, or what will happen if I can't get more.

☐ Lately I have been taking the drug more often or taking more of the drug at one time.

☐ I use the drug to help deal with my problems.

- [ ] My sleeping habits have changed—I sleep a lot more or a lot less than before I began using the drug.
- [ ] My grades have fallen since I began using, or I have been missing/skipping school.
- [ ] My behavior has changed. I feel less patient with family and friends and fall into arguments more often.
- [ ] I don't get as much exercise as I used to or spend as much time outside.
- [ ] I find it easier to be alone than with my usual friends or family, or I hang out with people who use my drug of choice because they understand me.
- [ ] I take more risks, such as driving after using or riding with someone who is high, having unprotected sex, using OxyContin with a needle, or mixing Vicodin or OxyContin with other drugs or alcohol.

Also, be sure you can recognize and respond to the warning signs of opioid overdose. Immediately call 911 if your friend shows any of these symptoms:

- cold, clammy skin
- confusion
- dangerously slow breathing
- seizures
- chest pain
- loss of consciousness

You Are the Key

Law enforcement can do only so much to prevent drug abuse. Perhaps the most important influence is education. Young people need to understand why Vicodin and OxyContin are so risky. Education begins with honest discussions between parents and children—even if those talks are embarrassing or difficult. The DEA confirms that young people who learn a lot about the risks of drugs from their parents are up to 50 percent less likely to use drugs. With that knowledge, you become the real key to stopping the cycle of drug abuse.

Kids are far less likely to use drugs if their parents talk to them about the risks.

Drugs may seem especially tempting when you feel stressed or lonely. In this situation communication becomes important. If you face a crisis, don't escape into drugs. There is always someone to help you. If you don't feel comfortable talking with a parent, look to another family member, friend, teacher, or spiritual leader who will understand. Seek out a support group or call a hotline. A few resources are listed in the Find Out More section in the back of this book. No matter how difficult things feel now, you'll be glad you didn't give away your future to drugs.

To move beyond these low points, look for positive outlets rather than escapes. Build (or rebuild) strong relationships with people around you. Even one positive, caring person can make all the difference in your life. Get involved in groups with people who share healthy and creative interests. Don't forget to stay active and fit. Drugs are less appealing when you feel healthy, connected, and fulfilled.

Even when life seems to be going fine, teens sometimes take risks to test their independence. New, challenging experiences can help you discover skills and interests you never expected. Keep in mind that it's not necessary to endanger your health while finding your path. The DEA

Leading a productive, active, and healthy life is a positive way to avoid drugs.

recommends that you give firm but friendly answers when someone invites (or pushes) you to try drugs. Sometimes all you have to do is say, "No, I'm not into that." Friends will find it hard to criticize you when you tell them, "No, I'm trying to stay healthy for [*fill in the name of a sport or other activity*]." "No thanks, I don't like how it makes people not act like themselves" are words that might inspire others to think about their own choices.

The Last Word

Using drugs might create the temporary illusion that your troubles have disappeared. One thing is certain: they will return as soon as you stop using. Often your problems become worse along the way. Opioids not only cause physical changes to your body, but also alter your behavior. The wake-up call to stop using does not always come from you. Vicodin and OxyContin abusers are sometimes sent to prison or rehab after being caught stealing drugs or money. They sometimes injure themselves or others because they were driving when high. Accidental overdose is common, and many other health risks come with long-term drug abuse.

There's no way to tell what your fate would be, even with a single use of Vicodin or OxyContin. Why take the chance? When faced with the suggestion to try a drug for fun, make a truly independent choice to be healthy instead. The joys of life—and even its pain and sorrows—are worth experiencing with a clear head.

Glossary

acute pain pain that feels intense but eases with healing

addictive tending to cause addiction

barbiturates a group of drugs more commonly known as sleeping pills

brand the name given to a particular product by the manufacturer

chronic pain frequently recurring or long-lasting pain

constrict to tighten up or make narrow

dependent reliant on something, such as a drug, for emotional and physical needs

depressant any type of drug that slows down bodily functions, such as breathing

endorphin a chemical produced in the body in response to pain

generic describing a drug without a brand name

illicit drugs those made illegal under federal law

nonprescription analgesic a painkilling drug available over the counter

opioid a painkilling drug made from opium or similar chemicals

opium a drug, obtained from particular poppy plants, which contains morphine and other chemicals that cause users to feel numb, sleepy, and muddled

overdose a large dose of a substance that causes a dangerous reaction in the body

rehabilitation a process of therapy and other help to overcome drug addiction

tolerance a reduction in the normal effects of a drug after regular use, requiring a larger dose to obtain the same effect

withdrawal the syndrome of symptoms that occur when a person who is physically dependent stops using a drug

Find Out More

BOOKS

Marshall Cavendish Reference. *Drugs of Abuse*. New York: Marshall Cavendish Reference, 2012.

———. *Substance Abuse, Addiction, and Treatment*. New York: Marshall Cavendish Reference, 2012.

Ramen, Fred. *Prescription Drugs*. New York: Rosen, 2007.

Slade, Suzanne. *OxyContin Abuse*. New York: Rosen Central, 2008.

Walker, Ida. *Painkillers: Prescription Dependency*. Philadelphia: Mason Crest, 2008.

WEBSITES

Center for Substance Abuse Treatment (CSAT)
www.samhsa.gov/about/csat.aspx
> CSAT helps individuals and families find substance abuse treatment programs in their communities.

Just Think Twice
www.justthinktwice.com/
> Prepared especially for kids by the Drug Enforcement Agency, this site provides information about a variety

of drugs commonly abused by teens and offers links
for those seeking support or treatment.

Nar-Anon and Nar-Ateen

www.nar-anon.org/

These organizations offer support for the family
and friends of people addicted to drugs. Nar-Ateen
meetings are especially for young people aged twelve
to twenty.

The Science behind Drug Abuse

http://teens.drugabuse.gov/

This site from the National Institute on Drug Abuse
looks specifically at the effects of drugs on the brain
and body.

Index

Pages in **boldface** are illustrations.

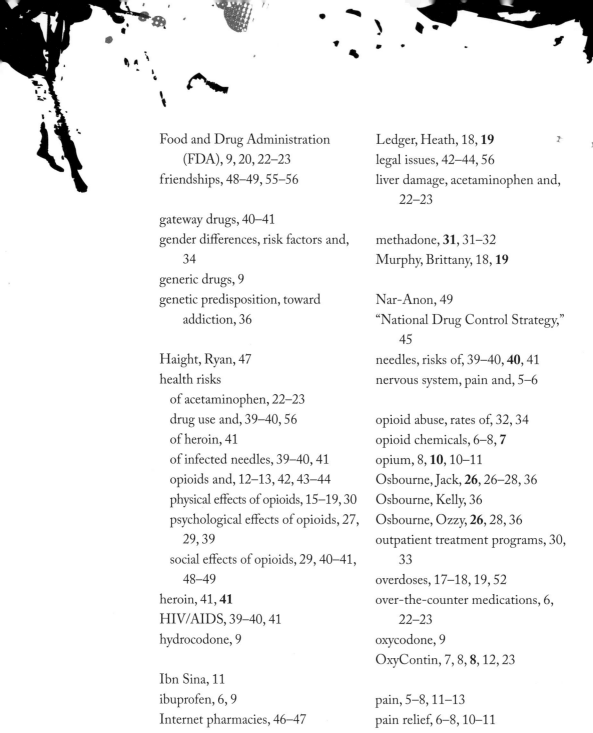

About the Author

Before becoming a freelance writer, **CHRISTINE PETERSEN** was a middle school science teacher. She has written more than forty books for young people, covering a wide range of topics in science, health, and social studies. When she is not writing, she and her son enjoy exploring the natural areas near their home in Minneapolis, Minnesota. She is a member of the Society of Children's Book Writers and Illustrators.